Table of Contents

Introduction

During the past several decades, military historians and theorists have produced numerous volumes of work on the topic of an American way of war. Historian Russell Weigley conducted the first serious attempt at examining America's approach to war in 1973.[1] Since then numerous authors have wrestled with the concept, providing multiple characterizations of the America methodology of war. Within this body of work, authors have attempted to codify characteristics that depict how Americans approach and conduct war. These works have often appeared, at first glance, diametrically opposed, providing characteristics of an American way of war that contradict one another.

Two challenges exist in attempting to define a singular American way of war. The first challenge lies in the broad scope of activities that the term encompasses. Douglas Lovelace, in the introduction to Antulio Echevarria's work on the topic, provides a definition of "a way of war" that demonstrates the tremendous scope of the subject. Lovelace contends, "A way of war implies thinking about conflict holistically, from prewar condition-setting to the final accomplishment of one's strategic objectives."[2] Brian Linn provides a similar definition in describing an institution's concept of war in his book *The Echo of Battle.* The concept, he claims, "encompasses tactics, operational methods, strategy, and all other factors that influence the preparation for, and conduct of, warfare."[3]

The second challenge to defining a singular American way of war exists because each conflict the United States has entered contained a unique set of circumstances and policy

---

[1] For a brief synopsis of the impact of Weigley's work within the military history community see Brian M. Linn, "The American Way of War Revisited," *The Journal of Military History* 66, no. 2 (April, 2002), 501-533.

[2] Douglas Lovelace, introduction to "Toward an American Way of War", by Antulio J. Echevarria, II, Strategic Studies Institute (March 2004), iii.

[3] Brian McAllister Linn, *The Echo of Battle: The Army's Way of War* (Cambridge: Harvard University Press, 2007), 233.

objectives. These objectives, in conjunction with the technological, material, and financial resources available to the military force at the time, shaped each conflict. As Clausewitz recognized, "every age had its own kind of war, its own limiting conditions, and its own peculiar preconceptions. Each period, therefore, would have held to its own theory of war, even if the urge had always and universally existed to work things out on scientific principles. It follows that the events of every age must be judged in the light of its own peculiarities."[4]

Although these challenges highlight the difficulty in generalizing an American way of war, they do help explain the accepted validity of apparently opposing accounts of the American military experience. Weigley claims that the United States possesses a way of war that is distinct from that of other Western societies. Using historical examples he argues that the United States has followed two primary strategies, one of attrition and one of annihilation. Weigley borrows from the work of Hans Delbruck in defining the strategy of annihilation as a strategy that "seeks the overthrow of the enemy's military power."[5] He draws upon Delbruck again to define the strategy of attrition; "which is usually employed by a strategist whose means are not great enough to permit pursuit of the direct overthrow of the enemy and who therefore resorts to an indirect approach."[6] Weigley's account of an American way of war that either pursued a strategy of annihilation or attrition appears contradictory to that offered by Max Boot in 2001which describes the United States' participation in small wars.

In his book *The Savage Wars of Peace,* Boot argues that the military history of the United States consists of more than just wars of attrition or annihilation. Boot claims that there is another

---

[4] Carl Von Clausewitz, *On War,* Trans. and ed. by Michael Howard and Peter Paret (Princeton, NJ: Princeton University Press, 1984), 593.

[5] Russell F. Weigley, *The American Way of War* (Bloomington: Indiana University Press, 1977), xxii.

[6] Ibid. Historian John Linn and military scholar Antulio Echevarria raise objections to Weigley's use of Delbruck's annihilation-attrition/exhaustion models. Both authors claim that Weigley confuses the definition throughout the book. Brian Linn, "The American Way of War Revisited", *The Journal of Military History,* Vol. 66, No. 2 (Apr., 2002), pp. 501-533 and Antulio J. Echevarria II, "Toward an American Way of War," Strategic Studies Institute, March 2004.

military tradition that has gone largely ignored; a tradition of small wars. In his book, he describes the numerous small wars the United States has conducted beginning with the Barbary Wars (1801-1805) through Vietnam (1959-1975). Boot identifies four distinct types of small wars: punitive (to punish attacks on American citizens or property), protective (to safeguard American citizens or property), pacification (to occupy foreign territory), and profiteering (to grab trade or territorial concessions)."[7] Boot claims that the United States' involvement in small wars contributed to the rise of the United States as a world power and warrant inclusion in any discussion on an American way of war.

In 2007, Brian McAllister Linn challenged both the views of Weigley and Boot in his book *The Echo of Battle.* Linn argues that trying to distill lessons from the study of military conduct on the battlefield provides a limited view of the American way of war. According to Linn, true appreciation of the concept "requires going beyond debates on the merits of attrition or annihilation, firepower or mobility, military genius or collective professional ability."[8] He argues that a true appreciation of the national way of war "requires the essential recognition that the way a military force conducts war very much depends on how it prepares for war."[9]

Linn divides the Army into three distinct intellectual groups whose thoughts combine to form the American Army's way of war. The first group dominated military thought for the majority of the nineteenth century. He calls this group the Guardians who see the primary goal of the military as deterring war. Guardians view war as a science and believe that through the leveraging of technological advantages and dominant maneuver the Army can achieve decisive victory. Linn calls the second group Heroes. Heroes see war as an art rather than a science. Victory for a Hero is the result of individual genius and inspiring leadership. Composing the last

---

[7] Max Boot, *The Savage Wars of Peace* (New York: Basic Books, 2002), xv-xvi.

[8] Linn, *The Echo of Battle*, 3.

[8] Ibid.

[9] Ibid.

group are Managers who see war as an organizational problem and believe success on the battlefield is dependent on efficient mobilization of massed armies. The three schools of thought attempt to predict future wars and prepare and organize the force to respond to the anticipated threat utilizing what they learned from past conflicts. According to Linn "a military institutions concept of war is a composite of its interpretation of the past, its perception of present threats, and its prediction of future hostilities."[10]

The accepted validity of these apparently opposing works demonstrates that an authoritative listing of characteristics that define an American way of war does not exist. Echevarria claims that although Weigley and Boot have different interpretations of the American tradition they do share a common characteristic. He argues that each author demonstrates that "the American way of war tends to shy away from thinking about the complicated process of turning military triumphs…into strategic success."[11] Echevarria asserts that instead of revealing that American's possess a way of war, these writings demonstrate that American's possess a way of battle.[12] Rather than deny an American way of war, Rose Keravuori claims that the American way of war is twofold. One is a strategic way of war, similar to that which Echaverria refers. Political concerns tie this way of war to the whims of a four-year political system and pressure an expedient military victory. When military and political outcomes do not align, victory may be independent of strategic policy success. The other way she defines as "a tactical way of battle" that involves a style of warfare in which distinct American attributes define the use of force. [13]

Keravuori's claims are consistent with the writings of Colin Gray. In *War, Peace, and International Relations,* Gray claims there is a distinct difference between war and warfare. War,

---

[10] Linn, *The Echo of Battle,* 233.

[11] Antulio J. Echevarria II, "Toward an American Way of War," Strategic Studies Institute (March 2004), vi.

[12] Ibid.

[13] Rose Lopez Keravuori, "Lost in Translation: "The American Way of War," *Small Wars Journal* (Nov 2011).

he argues, "is a legal concept, a social institution, and is a compound idea that embraces the total relationship between belligerents."[14] In contrast, "warfare refers to the actual conduct of war in its military dimension." In defining an American way of *war,* it would therefore be necessary to go beyond military thought and action and include the social, political, and economic conditions that effected how Americans prosecuted its wars. The characterization of the military aspect of war, including how the military thought about war during times of peace and practiced warfare during periods of conflict, is more aptly titled an American way of *warfare.*

These, and other, varied views on an American way of war highlight the difficulty of establishing universal and enduring principles that apply to a concept that contains numerous elements that vary with each manifestation.[15] However, this variety is the reason Antullio Echaverria accurately claims, "Boot's interpretation … complements rather than displaces Weigley's by broadening its focus" and Dr. Tom Bruscino proclaims Linn's work essential to the debate on the American way.[16]

Collectively, these works also represent the traditions of how the American military both conducts warfare during periods of conflict and thinks about war during periods of peace. When viewed holistically they provide insight into a set of general beliefs, attitudes, and behavioral patterns that characterize how Americans have fought over time. Where they fall short, as Bruscino points out, is in providing little insight into the reasons why Americans fought that way. Why did frontier wars against Native Americans so often turn into wars of extirpation? Why did Grant seek to annihilate the armies of the Confederacy? Why did America's small wars go largely

---

[14] Colin S. Gray, *War, Peace, and International Relations: An Introduction to Strategic History* (New York: Rutledge, 2007), 6.

[15] For a further review of the literature on an American way of war see Antulio Echevarria, "The American Way of War," in *A Companion to American Military History,* vol 2, ed. James C. Bradford (Oxford: Blackwell Publishing Ltd, 2010), 843-855.

[16] Echevarria, "Toward an American Way of War", 4.Thomas A. Bruscino, Jr. "Our American Mind for War." Review of *The Echo of Battle: The Army's Way of War* by Brian McAllister Linn, The Claremont Institute (May 26, 2008). http://www.claremont.org/publications/pub_print.asp?pubid=762 (accessed September 8, 2011).

ignored? Why do Guardians place their emphasis on deterrence, Heroes on charisma, and Managers on organization?[17]

It is the answer to these and similar questions that have driven the American operational approach to warfare, which in turn have shaped both the explicit and implicit doctrines and traditions that define the American way of warfare. In seeking the answer to these questions this monograph does not attempt to answer the why of *war* but rather the why of *warfare*. This monograph focuses on major Army operations and campaigns and explores the cultural influences that led commanders to conduct operations in the ways that they did. In doing so, this monograph aims to establish that over time, aspects of Army doctrine and operational traditions have achieved a state of semi-permanence. This enduring legacy represents an identifiable American way of warfare that encourages adaptive leaders to seek decisive victories through the application of superior power, which requires the ability to project that power over vast distances. It derives from the collective perceptions of historical military experience and influenced by the unique American experiences of geography, political philosophy, and civic culture.

This monograph will identify themes and consistencies in U.S. Army operations and campaigns and highlight those themes in Army doctrinal publications to identify changes and continuity to establish if there is such a thing as an American way of warfare. Using a model proposed by John Shy in an article titled "The American Military Experience: History and Learning" historical examples will be identified that demonstrate that these themes and consistencies have their roots in American's perception of their historical military experience. These historical experiences were themselves shaped by the unique American experiences of geography, political philosophy and civic culture.

---

[17] Bruscino argues that the underlying answer to all these questions lies in the fact that when the American citizenry mobilizes for war they demand quick victory. Thomas A. Bruscino, Jr. "Our American Mind for War." Review of *The Echo of Battle: The Army's Way of War* by Brian McAllister Linn. The Claremont Institute (May 26, 2008). http://www.claremont.org/publications/pub_print.asp?pubid=762 (accessed September 8, 2011).

Section II of this monograph discusses power projection and aspects of the American experience that gave rise to the requirement to deliberately plan and prepare for the conduct of military operations. The 1793 Battle of Fallen Timbers and 1863 Battle of Chattanooga provide examples that demonstrate that prior to 1898, military operations on the American continent where the culmination of deliberate and careful planning to overcome the vast distances and rugged terrain of the American frontier. Operation OVERLORD during World War II and Operation DESERT SHIELD in the 1990s demonstrate that the same requirements existed to overcome the United States' insular position.

Section III offers several examples of American colonial military operations that sought victory through the application of superior power. The colonial tendency to use superior force to defeat their enemies developed from American perceptions of their enemies, their high potential for military strength due to population and wealth of natural resources, and their lack of a professional standing army. American experiences during nineteenth century conflicts reinforced the tendency to seek victory through superior power. Military doctrine of the twentieth century made the tendency explicit and operations during World War II and Desert Storm show this tendency in action.

Section IV demonstrates that Americans inherited the desire for decisive victory from a broader western way of warfare that had its roots in Classical Greek history. Colonial military officers held the Western belief that the defeat of the enemy in decisive battle was the key to victory. The enemy force became the accepted objective and the destruction of the enemy force the goal. The tendency for Americans to view the world in Manichean terms reinforced this concept and twentieth century doctrine reflects this belief.

Section V examines the beginning of military organizations in colonial America to develop an understanding of the early cultural influences on American attitudes towards doctrine and discipline. The disdain for formal military discipline and lack of doctrine during the eighteenth and nineteenth centuries required adaptive leaders that were able to adapt doctrine and techniques to the realities of the enemy and terrain they confronted. This independent spirit and acceptance of ever-varying conditions is reflected in Army doctrine, which repeatedly claims that doctrine only serves as a guide for action.

In order to provide a framework for the methodology of this monograph, an overview of Shy's theory of history and learning is required. Shy challenged the practice of interpreting warfare through the lens of the science of military operations or as an instrument of national policy but rather he asserts that warfare is "a recurrent activity, always intense, sometimes traumatic, which closely touches national identity." He suggests that because of the episodic and traumatic characteristics of war, a society tends to remember only those features that it perceives, in some way, to control or dictate a successful response. Societies then tend to apply these remembered features to future situations it perceives to be similar.[18]

Shy borrows two hypotheses from learning theory to explain military behavior. The first is that infrequent situations are usually perceived utilizing a small number of "preferred cues"; the second is that complex situations are studied using a technique called "successive scanning." The term "preferred cues" refers to the tendency to reduce complex situations to only a few key features and "successive scanning" refers to the selection of information to reach "relatively simplistic conclusions."[19]

Using these two hypotheses Shy departs from a purely historical approach to study of war which holds that the "current significance of an event decreases directly with its distance in time from the present."[20] Rather Shy contends that priority, not proximity, in historical time should determine the importance of events.[21] The perceived similarity of current events to historical

---

[18] John Shy, "The American Military Experience: History and Learning," *The Journal of Interdisciplinary History,* Vol. 1, No. 2 (Winter, 1971), 208.

[19] Jerome S. Bruner, Jacqueline J. Goodnow, and George A. Austin, *A Study of Thinking* (New York: Wiley, 1956), 68-69 and 85-87.

[20] Shy, "The American Military Experience," 209.

[21] Ibid.

examples that produced positive results gives the historical event priority over other historical events that failed to produce a positive result irrespective of their proximity in time. In this view, the shared perception, memory, and behavior of a society over time can reveal coherence and consistency in what it learns from its remembered military past. This remembered military past, Shy assumes, "has always more or less constricted both action in the present and thinking about the future."[22]

This monograph recognizes that not every conflict in which the United States has participated will reflect all the themes presented. Rather what this monograph will attempt to demonstrate is that the United States military holds certain traditions that derive from a remembered military past. Over time, these traditions have achieved a state of semi-permanence and have become a part of both implicit and explicit doctrine and practice. A better understanding of these traditions will allow military practitioners to apply this understanding to concrete cases. As Colonel William Naylor stated in *The Principles of Strategy,* "In time of war, deeds play a more important part than words; action surpasses thought; practice dominates theory. It is not sufficient then merely to grasp principles: it is necessary to meditate upon them and to examine them thoroughly in their applications."[23]

Power Projection

Historian D.W. Brogan in his book *The American Character* claims that it was space, the vast distance of the frontier that determined how early Americans approached warfare. "Distance was the enemy, the great weapon of the Indian and of his allies, hunger and thirst."[24] The problem of opening up the frontier was that of establishing trails and roads, securing rivers that could float supplies, finding salt licks to rest and feed cattle, and identifying malaria free locations to make

---

[22] Shy, "The American Military Experience," 210.

[23] William K. Naylor, *Principles of Strategy with Historical Illustrations* (Fort Leavenworth, KS: The General Service Schools, 1921), 5.

[24] D.W. Brogan, *The American Character* (New York: Alfred A. Knopf, 1944), 152.

camps. Defeating this enemy required preparation, adequate planning, and the movement of required supplies and resources. Movement through the vast, unsettled wilderness of the American frontier had to, out of necessity, be more cautious and deliberate than traversing the relatively well-settled European continent.

In 1792, General "Mad" Anthony Wayne recognized this as his true enemy when President George Washington asked him to build a legion capable of defeating the Western Confederacy of Indian tribes in what is now the state of Ohio. Wayne realized that the failure of two previous expeditions into the region was due to inadequacies in planning for and establishing necessary supply points, inadequate training and preparation of the military force, and failing to protect the force as it moved through the wild country. Wayne highlighted his unwillingness to risk taking to the field unprepared in a note he sent to Secretary of War Henry Knox. He wrote Knox, "You may rest assured that I will not commit the Legion Unnecessarily & unless more powerfully supported than I at present have reason to expect."[25] Wayne spent the majority of 1793 preparing and training his force of nearly 3,000 men. As Wayne moved his legion north, he built a series of forts to protect his supply line and rear areas. As Brogan stated, "he prepared, with unsporting thoroughness, to move safely and in overwhelming force. Long before he won the Battle of Fallen Timbers, Wayne had won the war..."[26]

In both *The American Way of War* and *Eisenhower's Lieutenants*, Weigley stresses that Americans predominantly practiced a direct approach to warfare, using frontal assaults aimed at the destruction of the enemy. Often overlooked is the fact that the actual battle was the culmination of extensive planning and preparation and involved the movement of significant supplies, material, and personnel. During the Civil War, Union General Philip Sheridan exemplified the type of battle referred to by Weigley. At the battle of Chattanooga, Sheridan led

---

[25] Anthony Wayne quoted in Paul David Nelson, *Anthony Wayne: Soldier of the Early Republic* (Bloomington, IN: Indiana University Press, 1985), 244.

[26] Brogan, *The American Character*, 152.

10

his division up Missionary Ridge, directly into the Confederate rifle pits above, breaking the Confederate lines, and forcing Confederate General Braxton Bragg into retreat. However, Brogan points out that Sheridan's action, although dramatic, "was a mere finale to a long play." The battle's end result had been determine weeks before when Grant was able to open a line of supplies into Chattanooga "down which poured the endless resources of the North to be launched suddenly, when the issue was beyond all doubt, like an avalanche pouring uphill on the gallant, outnumbered, underequipped Southern army."[27]

Post-Civil War military theorists in the United States came to the realization that industrialization, the ability to mass produce uniforms, weapons, munitions, and food was necessary to support the recruitment, training, and transportation of the massive armies required to fight "modern wars." American military intellectuals such as Emory Upton and Arthur Wagner as well as military writers such as John Bigelow and Francis Greene believed that the conduct of modern warfare had profoundly changed because of industrialization. As Brian Linn observed, "The scale of industrialized warfare, the complexity of its weaponry, the coordination of transport and communications, the movement of tens of thousands of soldiers and their deployment into battle – all of these required managerial skills equivalent to those displayed by financial magnates and captains of industry."[28]

This line of reasoning gave rise to a managerial style of officer that Linn characterizes as seeing warfare as an organizational problem. Managers, according to Linn, believe that they can make war more effective through "the rational coordination of resources, both human and material".[29] However, the effective waging of war may not be the only reasoning behind a managerial philosophy toward warfare. As Brogan implies, the vast distances and rugged landscape that early Americans had to overcome made intensive management of military and

---

[27] Brogan, *The American Character*, 153

[28] Linn, *The Echo of Battle*, 52.

[29] Ibid., 8.

colonial operations a necessity. Behind pathfinders like Daniel Boone and Simon Kenton were businessmen like George Washington and Leland Standford who provided the financial and organizational capabilities required to conduct early expeditions. These men knew that conquering distance required resources and planning as well as men determined enough to face the hardships. Necessity drove these men to thoroughly plan and prepare their expeditions, the necessity to conquer distance and to coordinate the vast amount of resources required. These were the same necessities that drove Grant to plan and prepare as he did.

As the American frontier was closing and the distance between the east and west coasts were shrinking, America's role in world affairs was increasing. Its insular position no longer separated it from the affairs of the rest of the world. As the country entered into the 20th century, military planners realized that events in Europe could pose a security threat to the United States. The U.S. Army's 1936 version of *The Principles of Strategy* recognized that overseas expeditions were a potentiality and possessed unique requirements. Overseas expeditions require that "a base…must be established in the vicinity of a port of entry…The selection…depends on the plan of campaign, the location of suitable ports, and the facilities of movement available therefrom."[30] During World War II, these concerns would drive U.S. and allied planning efforts in preparation for the allied assault of the European continent against Nazi Germany. Again, distance would be a factor. However, instead of facing the vastness of a wild frontier, military planners at the start of World War II faced the challenge of crossing an ocean.

Planning, mobilization, preparation, and movement for Operation OVERLORD, whose objective was "to secure a lodgement area on the Continent from which further offensive operations could be developed," lasted several years.[31] The American Army of 1940, in the words of Weigley, was "not an Army in the European fashion, but a border constabulary for policing

---

[30] Command and General Staff School, *The Principles of Strategy for an Independent Corps* (Fort Leavenworth, KS: The Command and General Staff School Press, 1936), 30.

[31] Supreme Headquarters, Allied Expeditionary Forces, *SHAEF (44) 22, Operation OVERLORD*, March 10, 1944, 1.

unruly Indians and Mexicans."[32] It consisted of roughly 180,000 men and 12,000 to 13,000 officers. Over the course of the next three years, it would grow to an Army of 8,300,000.[33] These men had to be equipped, trained, and transported overseas in order to conduct operations on the continent of Europe. It required one of the largest mobilizations of an army the world had ever seen and it took years of planning and preparation to accomplish.

Throughout the remainder of the twentieth-century, the speed at which technological advances changed the nature of warfare increased dramatically. The atomic bomb, jet aircraft, and the computer revolution all served to make warfare faster and more deadly. Yet, in relative terms, the requirement to plan, prepare, mobilize, and transport American forces to the scene of conflicts remained unchanged. In 1990, the U.S. would again mount one of the largest build-ups of military forces the world had ever seen.

Since 1973, the American Army has consisted of an all-volunteer force, which alleviated the need to mobilize and train personnel for wartime service as in previous American conflicts. However, in 1990, as General Norman Schwarzkopf was preparing America's reaction to Iraq's invasion of Kuwait, he realized that he needed support soldiers "to take on the nitty-gritty tasks of supporting a deployment in a combat zone."[34] The forces that Schwarzkopf required belonged to the Army National Guard and Reserves. In utilizing Guard and Reserve soldiers Schwarzkopf faced the same concern of General Winfield Scott in his use of volunteer militia over one-hundred fifty years before; mobilizing reserve forces would take time and they would only be available to the commander for a limited time. As Schwarzkopf noted, "by the time we sent them to the Middle East, I'd have to worry about bringing them home."[35]

---

[32] Russell F. Weigley, *Eisenhower's Lieutenants: The Campaign of France and Germany 1944-1945* (Bloomington: Indiana University Press, 1981), 2.

[33] Ibid., 10.

[34] H. Norman Schwarzkopf, *It Doesn't Take a Hero* (New York: Bantam Books, 1992), 323.

[35] Ibid.

The tailored force that Schwarzkopf required for Operation Desert Shield/Desert Storm consisted of 140,000 Army guardsmen and reservists and 160,000 full-time soldiers. The mobilization and deployment process involved deploying the equivalent of eight Army divisions, all of their equipment, and 60 days of supply. This force-projection operation would last six months and required the planning and coordination of all U.S. Armed services.[36]

The 1993 version of FM 100-5 recognized the lessons learned from this deployment and highlights the challenges and complexity of projecting a modern force overseas. It states, "Force projection is a complex process in which each action impacts upon many others. The commander and the force will routinely be required to plan execute multiple concurrent activities. Decisions made early will begin to set conditions for successful mission accomplishment."[37] This warning is as applicable to the actions and decisions of General Wayne in the 1793 or Grant in 1863 as to General Schwarzkopf in 1991.

Over time conditions effecting America's conflicts have changed, but a consistency remains; when America decides to use military force it must be willing and able to project power across vast distances. From early colonial and Civil War commanders operating in the interior of the United States to global operations during the 20th Century, when the U.S. has decided to use military power to pursue policy objectives, that power had to be projected across vast distances. This power projection was carefully planned, deliberately executed, and involved the mobilization of personnel and resources. An often-used quote erroneously ascribed to General Nathan Bedford Forrest provides a succinct condensation for the purpose of this American tradition, to "git thar fustest with mostest."

---

[36] For a complete description of deployment operations, including unit designations and deployment timelines see Center for Military History, *War in the Persian Gulf: Operations Desert Shield and Desert Strom August 1990 - March 1991* (Washington, D.C.: U.S. Army Center for Military History, 2010).

[37] U.S. Department of the Army, *Field Manual 100-5: Operations* (Washington, D.C.: Headquarters Department of the Army, 1993), 3-3.

Superior Power and the Principle of Mass

Russell Weigley claims that the U.S. Army of the 1940s had inherited certain traditions from the U.S. Civil War and the actions of the Union Commander, General Ulysses S. Grant. Grant's method of defeating the brilliant maneuverings of the Confederate Commander, General Robert E. Lee, was to exploit the North's superior numbers and resources to lock the South into continuous battle. In other words, Grant defeated the Confederacy "by drowning its armies in a flood of overwhelming power."[38] Grant's success reinforced the Army's belief that the primary means of victory in any major conflict was through the application of overwhelming superior power to destroy the enemy's military force, the enemy's economy, and its will to fight.

British historian D.W. Brogan claims that the tradition of superior power dates back to earlier American experiences encountered while conquering the vast American continent. Beginning with early colonization, American settlers had to face native enemies that were intimately familiar with every nuance of the terrain, the possibilities and dangers of the environment, and the routes and trails necessary for quick and safe navigation. Many of the native inhabitants were highly militarized and could only be conquered "by patience, prudence, and massing of superior resources."[39]

Brogan cites several examples of colonial military failures and successes including George Washington's surrender at Fort Necessity and British Major General Edward Braddock's failed expedition to retake the fort from the French. The "parade ground virtues," of the English army could not defeat the "more forest-wise" French and their Indian allies. Through observing the actions of British regulars, early colonists came to believe that war was not "the sport of kings" but rather a serious national and personal concern. Being reckless could cost an individual

---

[38] Weigley, *Eisenhower's Lieutenants*, 3.

[39] Brogan, *The American Character,* 150.

his scalp; the victorious survived "by logistics, by superiority in resources…in numbers."[40] The

Continental Army quickly learned and applied these lessons.

The 1779 Clinton-Sullivan Campaign against the Iroquois nation in New York is an

example of such a lesson. In 1778, British Loyalist John Butler established a force of colonial

Rangers and Indian warriors from the Iroquois tribe to attack and lay waste to Patriot settlements

along the Northern frontier of New York. Along with a band of Mohawks under the leadership of

Joseph Brant, loyalists and Indians devastated Patriot colonists through the first half of 1779. In

the early part of that year, the Continental Congress determined that the problem demanded that

"an army of overwhelming strength" sweep across northern New York to drive the Indians to

"seek habitations where they would be less troublesome."[41]

John Grenier called the resulting operation "one of the most complex American

operations of the War of Independence."[42] It consisted of three separate armies, one under Major

General John Sullivan, another under Brigadier General James Clinton, and the last under

Colonel Daniel Brodhead. The three armies spent the summer clearing northern New York of

Seneca and Mohawk Indian villages.

The ability to mass superior power, either in terms of personnel, in terms of resources, or

both, existed in America from the time of the early colonies. Although the colonies did not

possess a standing army, John Shy points out that as colonies became more heavily and densely

populated they acquired a high military potential "much greater than that of even the strongest

Indian tribes."[43] Brogan claims America is a country of "lavish natural wealth and lavish artificial

---

[40] Brogan, *The American Character,* 150.

[41] John Grenier, *The First Way of War: American War Making on the Frontier, 1607-1814* (Cambridge: Cambridge University Press, 2005), 166-167.

[42] Ibid., 166.

[43] Shy, "The American Military Experience," 213.

wealth created by its own efforts." This wealth enables American military efforts to win "by their mere scale and by their ability to wait until that scale tells."[44]

Both military theory and the Army's Operational doctrine of the 1920s, 1930s and 1940s reflect the primacy of superior power. In Colonel William Naylor's 1921 *Principles of Strategy,* he states that tactical superiority is the precondition for success. "It is a general principle of all combat to be stronger at the critical point than the enemy."[45] The 1936 version of *The Principles of Strategy for An Independent Corps or Army in a Theater of Operations* published by the Army's Command and General Staff School also stressed that "where the quality of troops and leadership is about the same on both sides, numerical superiority generally determines the result"[46]

The first publication of FM 100-5 in 1939 by the U.S. War Department reflects Naylor's sentiments. The 1939 manual states, "Concentration of *superior forces*, both on the ground and in the air, at the decisive place and time, creates the conditions most essential to decisive victory."[47] Both the 1941 and 1944 versions place the same emphasis on "concentration of superior forces" in the creation of the conditions necessary for victory.

The military planners of Operation NEPTUNE during World War II felt that overwhelming superiority was a necessity in establishing a foothold on the Normandy coast. They recognized their basic problem was to establish and maintain a reasonable margin of superiority over the enemy.[48] Prior to General Eisenhower's appointment as the Supreme Allied Commander, the Chief of Staff, Supreme Allied Commander (COSSAC) planners had to contend with severe

---

[44] Brogan, *The American Character,* 162-163.

[45] Naylor, *Principles of Strategy With Historical Illustrations*, 26.

[46] The Command and General Staff School, *The Principles of Strategy for an Independent Corps or Army in a Theater of Operations* (Fort Leavenworth, KS: The Command and General Staff School Press, 1936), 17.

[47] U.S. War Department, *Field Service Regulation, FM 100-5: Operations* (Washington D.C.: Government Printing Office, 1939), 27.

[48] Gordon A. Harrison, *Cross-Channel Attack* (Washington, D.C.: U.S. Army Center of Military History, 1993), 74.

resource restrictions as a result of Allied operations in the Mediterranean. They faced a shortage of both personnel and resources, especially in the number of amphibious landing craft necessary to move the ground forces across the channel. One COSSAC planner claimed that the shortage of landing craft required to move a force superior to the German defenders "can readily be made the excuse for failure to do operations which otherwise might prove practical."[49]

Throughout the early planning of the operation, the COSSAC planning staff and the American Joint Chiefs of Staff debated the number of divisions required and the number of landing craft necessary to support the invasion.. However, U.S. industrial ability to produce craft capable of 106,146 light displacement tons in 1942 and maintain a production of 60,000 tons monthly through the first half of 1944, reflect the economic might that the Americans brought to the war effort.[50] This industrial might enabled the allies to amass the required superior power deemed necessary to conduct such a bold cross-Channel attack. As Weigley summarized, "The immense resources of the twentieth-century United States continued to reinforce the appropriateness of such means to this nation's warmaking."[51]

Military doctrine after World War II continued to reflect the American penchant for using superior power in the conduct of warfare. The 1949 version of FM 100-5 states that one of the principles of war is mass and adds it to the statement on concentration of superior forces found in the 1944 version of the manual. The 1949 version reads, "Mass or the concentration of superior forces, on the ground, at sea, and in the air, at the decisive place and time, and their employment in a decisive direction, creates the conditions essential to victory"[52] The 1954 version of the manual places greater emphasis on the principle of mass. "Maximum available combat power must be applied at the point of decision. Mass is the concentration of means at the critical time

---

[49] Harrison, *Cross-Channel Attack*, 60.

[50] Ibid., 62-63.

[51] Weigley, *Eisenhower's Lieutenants*, 3.

[52] U.S. Department of the Army, *Field Service Regulation, FM 100-5: Operations* (Washington D.C.: U.S. Government Printing Office, 1949), 28.

and place to the maximum degree permitted by the situation." It clarifies that numbers alone does not achieve mass rather "a combination of manpower and firepower" and "may permit numerically inferior forces to achieve decisive combat superiority."[53]

The basic concept of the principle of mass changed very little in Army doctrine until the publication of FM 100-5 in 1993. The 1993 version explicitly links mass and combat power, expanding combat power to include elements of maneuver, firepower, protection, and leadership. The 1993 publication states that mass is achieved through "Synchronizing all elements of combat power where they will have decisive effect on an enemy force in a short period of time…"[54]

In a 2006 study of the American way of war by the Center for Naval Analyses (CNA) Corporation, H.H. Gafney states, "The U.S. has believed in applying overwhelming force to solve a situation—a concept that might be regarded as something more than might otherwise be considered appropriate." As an example, he cites the plan to build up forces during the 1991 Gulf War that matched the size of the Iraqi army and to provide the Allied ground forces with enough ammunition to support 30 days of combat operations.[55]

In October of 1990, General Schwarzkopf's planning staff briefed the President and National Security advisors on the plan for a ground attack to liberate Kuwait from the control of Saddam Hussein. Schwarzkopf was uncomfortable with conducting a full-scale counterattack with the forces he had available at the time saying, "Even if we succeeded in seizing the highway junction, Iraq could throw its huge army north of Kuwait against us in a counterattack. A battle of attrition would follow, in which Iraq's numerical superiority would give it a decided advantage."[56] Schwarzkopf said that the "textbook" way to defeat a force in a fixed defensive

---

[53] U.S. Department of the Army, *Field Service Regulation, FM 100-5: Operations* (Washington D.C.: U.S. Government Printing Office, 1954), 26.

[54] U.S. Department of the Army, *Field Manual 100-5: Operations* (Washington, D.C.: Headquarters Department of the Army, 1993), 2-4.

[55] H.H. Gafney, "The American Way of War Through 2020" (Alexandria, VA: Center for Strategic Studies, CNA Corporation, 2006), 12.

[56] Schwarzkopf, *It Doesn't Take a Hero*, 356.

position, as the Iraqi Army in Kuwait, was to fix the force in place with a frontal attack while sending a superior force to "outflank it, envelop it, and crush it against the sea." To do this Schwarzkopf told the President he needed an additional Armored Corps consisting of two armored divisions.

General Schwarzkopf had to wait nearly a month before he received word that the President had approved his request for additional forces. In fact, the President had authorized the deployment of forces in excess of what Schwarzkopf had asked for. Instead of the two divisions that he requested, he would receive three with an additional armored brigade as well as an additional division of Marines. All of this, in the words of the President, was to ensure "an adequate offensive military operation."[57]

As both Brogan and Weigley observed, America has possessed both the natural resources and economic capability to support military commanders with the ability to achieve superior power in material and resources. This characteristic has provided the American military advantages in the conduct of large-scale, force on force conflicts. The goal of this type of warfare has been to bring the enemy's force into battle and rapidly defeat them in a decisive manner. Historian Victor Davis Hanson argues that this is not a purely American trait.

Decisive Victory and the Direct Approach

In *Carnage and Culture: Landmark Battles in the Rise of Western Power,* Hanson asserts that decisive battles are characteristic of an enduring Western way of war that originated with the classical Greeks. Hanson argues that the concepts of a Western style of warfare developed in the Greek city-states. Small Greek communities were self-sustaining and governed by the private landholders who cultivated the land that surrounded it. These free landholders voted on the decision to go to war to either win property or protect their territory. The landholders were also the infantrymen that comprised the armies that would conduct the battle. To these men the most

---

[57] Schwarzkopf, *It Doesn't Take a Hero,* 376.

economical way to wage war was to "muster the largest, best-armed group of farmers to protect land in the quickest, cheapest, and most decisive way possible."[58]According to Hanson, these men desired a method of battle that was quick and provided a clear-cut victor. These circumstances led to a Western tradition of seeking decisive battles.

Western military thought influenced early American conduct of warfare. Modeling the martial thought of the classic Greeks, Americans feared that a large standing army was a threat to the liberty of free peoples. Samuel Adams reflected this sentiment in 1768 stating, "It is a very improbable supposition, that any people can long remain free, with a strong military power in the heart of their country."[59] Most American's believed that a well-trained militia, composed of free citizens, was the proper and natural way to defend a free state. Keravuori argues that the imbuement of the Greek ideals of consensual government and the Greek form of fighting led to an American penchant for decisive battle. Similar to ancient Greeks, early Americans sought a clear, rapid resolution to disputes that minimized time and lives lost. For early Americans, war was a disruption to their daily lives and, according to Shy, meant inevitable and often horrible death and suffering.[60]

Both Shy and Weigley argue that despite their shared traditions and history, American and European methods of warfare took different directions in the mid-seventeenth century. After the end of the Thirty Years War (1618-1648), Europeans gradually progressed to a more rational or restrained type of conflict known as limited warfare. However, early American colonists continued to pursue the total destruction of their enemies as the purpose of conflict. Expanding on Shy's concepts, Don Higginbotham claims that this occurred for two reasons. The first reason was that, at least until the War of 1812, early Americans were fighting for their very survival,

---

[58] Victor Davis Hanson, *Carnage and Culture: Landmark Battles in the Rise of Western Power* (New York: Anchor Books, 2001), 92.

[59] Samuel Adams, quoted in Marcus Cunliffe, *Soldiers and Civilians: The Martial Spirit in America 1772-1865* (New York: The Free Press, 1973), 29.

[60] Shy, "The American Military Experience," 214.

both militarily and politically. The second was that the enemies of the colonists were either heathen "savages" or hated French and Spanish "papists."[61] Shy states that American Colonists were "highly vulnerable, angered, and frightened by repeated attack, bewildered by the causes of war, disrupted by its effects, and powerless to prevent it."[62] Both Shy and Higginbotham claim these experiences led Americans to seek a definitive military solution leading to the total removal of their enemies from the continent. "Anything less was worse than useless, because it would create a false sense of security."[63]

John Grenier in his book *The First Way of War* claims that colonial warfare consisted primarily of non-professional soldiers using irregular means to pursue unlimited objectives. Warfare often manifested in what Grenier called, "patterns of extravagant violence and *petite guerre.*"[64] The American tradition of warfare that developed was a combination of traditional European and Native American methods. These characteristics arose, at least in part, from how Americans viewed both their environment and themselves. Historian John Ferling argued that the rugged realities of the wilderness and a racist attitude towards the native population led to a tradition of "unique brutality" in early American warfare.[65] Ronald Dale Karr suggests that early colonists failed to see the natives as sovereign and treated the Indians like rebels, heretics, or infidels.[66] It was these views, according to Grenier, that caused Americans to seek extirpating Indians. Two years after Shy published his article, Weigley published *The American Way of War* in which he characterized the American way of war after 1815 as emphasizing the pursuit of a strategy of annihilation. According to Weigley, when the American military pursued a strategy

---

[61] Don Higginbotham, "The Early American Way of War: Reconnaissance and Appraisal," *The William and Mary Quarterly,* Third Series, Vol. 44, No. 2 (April, 1987), 231.

[62] Shy, "The American Military Experience," 214.

[63] Ibid.

[64] Grenier, *The First Way of War*, 6.

[65] John Ferling, *A Wilderness of Miseries: War and Warriors in Early America* (Westport, CT: Greenwood Press, 1980), 17.

[66] Ronald Dale Karr, "Why Should You Be So Ferocious?: The Violence of the Pequot War," *Journal of American History*, 85 (1999), 908-909.

other than that of annihilation they did so only because they did not possess the necessary strength to do otherwise. Shy argues that the lack of a strong, professional military contributed to colonial American's pursuit of a "complete solution" in dealing with their enemies. Because war was so costly and disruptive to a colonial society whose military consisted of the civil population, absolute victory was the only way to guarantee the safety of society who would not or could not maintain a standing military force.[67]

Also contributing to the American tendency to pursue the destruction of their enemy as the primary objective is an enduring tendency to view the world in Manichean terms. President George W. Bush provided a poignant example of this tendency during a 2001 Address to a Joint Session of Congress and the American People. Responding the events of September 11, 2001, the President told the world, "Either you are with us, or you are with the terrorists."[68] As with the military reaction to the terrorist's attacks at the World Trade Center and the Pentagon, Americans have been able to justify military action in terms of perceived criminal conduct of an immoral or evil foe. From an American perspective, dealing with such enemies requires decisive action. In the words of President Franklin Roosevelt, "There never has been and never can be a successful compromise between good and evil. Only total victory can reward the champions of tolerance and decency and freedom and faith."[69]

Shy claims that despite America's lack of a strong standing army, when early Americans made the decision to mobilize for conflicts, they possessed a high potential for military strength. The abundant natural resources and booming population growth in the United States during the nineteenth century supplied the necessary resources for the continued pursuit of decisive victory through defeat of the enemy army. Shy also argues that the military experiences of the United

---

[67] Higginbotham, "The Early American Way of War," 232.

[68] George W. Bush, "Address to a Joint Session of Congress and the American People, September 20, 2001," The White House, http://georgewbush-whitehouse.archives.gov/news/releases/2001/09/20010920-8.html (accessed January 3, 2012).

[69] Franklin D. Roosevelt, *The American Way: Selections from the Public Addresses and Papers of Franklin D. Roosevelt,* edited by Dagobert D.Runes (New York: Philosophical Library, 1944), 22.

States during the nineteenth century did little to change this existing attitude. He claims that the Seminole Wars, the Mexican-American War, the Indian Wars, and the Spanish-American War reinforced American beliefs that they could achieve decisive victories with minimal cost. He points out that each of these wars ended with the extension of American territory and control and, although not the conscious political objectives, these positive "natural rewards" served to reinforce existing American attitudes towards warfare.

American military thinkers after World War I began establishing principles of war intended to provide guidance to military officers in the fundamentals of successful military operations. The principle of the objective consistently appeared first and had special significance. Weigley summarized the principle as "the truism that every military operation should be directed toward a decisive and attainable objective."[70] Colonel Naylor made this his first principle of strategy which stated, "Make the hostile main army the objective." Again, Army doctrine would echo Naylor's sentiments. The 1939 version of FM 100-5 states, "The primary objective of all military operations is the destruction of the enemy's armed forces in battle."[71] The 1941 version of the manual also highlights the importance of objective to decisive victory. It states that an able commander has "the ability to select objectives whose attainment contributes most decisively and quickly to the defeat of the hostile armed forces."[72] Like the 1939 version, the 1941 version of the FM 100-5 stresses, "the ultimate objective of all military operations is the destruction of the enemy's armed forces in battle."[73]

During the American-British Conversations 1 (ABC-1) in early 1941, British and American strategists discussed the appropriate strategy that the Allies should pursue if the United

---

[70] Weigley, *Eisenhower's Lieutenants*, 3-4.

[71] U.S. War Department, *Field Service Regulation, FM 100-5: Operations* (Washington D.C.: Government Printing Office, 1939), 27.

[72] U.S. War Department, *Field Service Regulation, FM 100-5: Operations* (Washington D.C.: Government Printing Office, 1941), 22.

[73] Ibid.

States entered the war against a German-Italian-Japanese Axis. Consistent with the American tradition of seeking decisive victory through the destruction of the enemy's army, American strategists believed that the allies should "assail the main armed strength of the enemy directly, to destroy that strength."[74] The War Plans Division echoed this sentiment. In a memorandum outlining the ultimate requirements for the war, Major Albert C. Wedemeyer stated, "Irrespective of the scope and nature of these operations, we must prepare to fight Germany by actually coming to grips with and defeating her ground forces and definitely breaking her will to combat."[75]

The strategy desired by the British highlights the difference in the American and British approaches to warfare during this time. The British desired to pursue a more indirect approach aimed at positions of German weakness, such as in the Mediterranean, in an attempt to erode German strength. They felt that an assault against the enemy's Fortress Europe would be unsuccessful, or too costly if successful, until the allies had sufficiently eroded German strength. British military theorists B.H. Liddell Hart described this approach in his book *Strategy*. He stated that in modern war "the true aim is not so much to seek battle as to seek a strategic situation so advantageous that if it does not of itself produce the decision, its continuation by a battle is sure to achieve this."[76] The 1925 General Service School's *Review of Current Military Literature* revealed American attitudes towards Hart's ideas stating that they were "Of negative value to the instructors at these schools."[77] This statement reflected Naylor's *Principles of Strategy* in which he wrote that victory without battle could not achieve the purpose of modern war, which was to seek the complete overthrow or annihilation of the enemy.[78]

---

[74] Weigley, *Eisenhower's Lieutenants*, 7.

[75] Albert C. Wedemeyer, "WPD Memorandum, Ultimate Requirements--Ground forces, 23 August 1941," quoted in Charles E. Kirkpatrick, *An Unknown Future and a Doubtful Present: Writing the Victory Plan of 1941* (Washington, D.C.: Center for Military History, 1992), 64.

[76] B.H. Liddell Hart, *Strategy* (New York: Frederick A Praeger, 1954), 365.

[77] The General Service Schools, review of *Paris, or the Future of War*, by B.H. Liddell Hart, *Review of Current Military Writings* no. 19 (October-December, 1925): 20.

[78] Naylor, *Principles of Strategy*, 35.

Since the 1950's, the American military has had several strategic policies that have shaped how the military is organized and equipped to fight. These include the strategy of 'flexible response" ushered in by President John F. Kennedy in 1961, "active defense" which was introduced in the 1976 version of *Field Manual 100-5*, "air-land battle" with the publication of the 1982 version, and the current doctrine of "unified land operations" published in *Army Doctrine Publication 3.0.* Although each of these doctrinal publications describes warfare in different ways and organizes the Army differently, one concept remains constant: the U.S Army seeks a direct approach and prefers decisive action.

The 1962 version of FM 100-5 clearly articulates this fact. It states, "Every military operation must be directed toward a clearly defined, decisive and attainable objective. The ultimate military objective of war is the destruction of the enemy's armed forces and his will to fight."[79] The AirLand Battle doctrine in 1982 version of the manual departs from the clear statements of previous manuals. However, a careful reading still highlights the tradition of decisive action focused on the enemy force. It states, "The AirLand Battle will be dominated by the force that retains the initiative and, with deep attack and decisive maneuver, destroys its opponent's abilities to fight and to organize in depth."[80] The 1986 version returns to the centrality of the destruction of the enemy stating, "The object of all operations is to destroy the opposing force."[81] The 1993 version of the manual recognized that the ability of the Army to "respond quickly and decisively to global requirements is fundamental to Army operations doctrine" with the overall strategic aim being "decisive land combat."[82] It also specified that the Army's ability

---

[79] Department of the Army, *Field Service Regulation, FM 100-5: Operations* (Washington, D.C.: Headquarters Department of the Army, 1962), 46.

[80] Department of the Army, *Field Manual 100-5: Operations* (Washington, D.C.: Headquarters Department of the Army, 1982), 1-5.

[81] Department of the Army, *Field Manual 100-5: Operations* (Washington, D.C.: Headquarters Department of the Army, 1986), 2-1.

[82] Department of the Army, *Field Manual 100-5: Operations* (Washington, D.C.: Headquarters Department of the Army, 1993), iv.

to conduct "sustained land operations" is what makes it a decisive force.[83] ADP 3.0 states that the Army achieves "decisive and sustainable land operations through the simultaneous combination of offensive, defensive, and stability operations."[84] The manual also recognizes an expanded role of Army operations but includes the ability "to defeat or destroy an enemy" as one of its tasks.[85] Although the pursuit of victory through the defeat of the enemy army in a single decisive battle is rarely an operational reality on the modern battlefield, the tradition of seeking decisive action and the pursuit of the destruction of the enemy force has been a constant theme in Army doctrine.

Leadership, the American Spirit and the Tenet of Adaptability

On 23 February 1778, Frederich von Stueben arrived at Valley Forge Pennsylvania to train Washington's Continental Army on military drill. Washington hoped that Steuben, an experienced Prussian military officer turned mercenary, and others like him could assist in arranging, training, and fitting the Continental Army for the upcoming campaign season.[86] However, some of Washington's Colonial officers distrusted European military officers especially a Prussian automaton. One Colonial officer, Colonel Timothy Pickering, believed that European style drill had no place in an American military culture, claiming, "Tis the boast of some that their men are machines, but God forbid that my countrymen should ever be thus degraded."[87]Pickering's sentiments reflected a martial tradition established by earlier colonials.

Prior to the American Revolutionary War, colonial military forces followed informal styles of warfare without the benefit of explicit regulations or military doctrine. Despite their lack

---

[83] Department of the Army, *Field Manual 100-5: Operations* (Washington, D.C.: Headquarters Department of the Army, 1993), 1-4.

[84] Department of the Army, *Army Doctrine Publication 3-0: Unified Land Operations* (Washington D.C.: Headquarters Department of the Army, 2011), 5.

[85] Ibid.

[86] Walter E. Kretchik, *U.S. Army Doctrine: From the American Revolution to the War on Terror* (Lawrence, KS: University Press of Kansas, 2011), 16-17.

[87] Timothy Pickering, *An Easy Plan of Discipline for a Militia* (Salem, MA: Samuel and Ebenezer Hall, 1775), xi.

of formal doctrine, local militia companies trained utilizing locally developed tactics, techniques, and procedures. For the most part, local militias garnered their methods from European military writings and word-of-mouth instruction from mercenaries who had experience in European style linear warfare.[88] Most colonials rejected conventional European military tactics because they were not suited to the terrain and the style of warfare practiced by their primary adversary, Native American Indians. Indians practiced a way of war that early settlers called "skulking". Grenier characterized skulking as the Indian's "ability to capitalize on speed and stealth to strike and retreat out of harm's way."[89] Early colonist Nathaniel Saltonstall described the challenge of fighting the Indians by describing them as "being so light of foot that they can run away when they list, and pass Bogs, rocky Mountains and thickets, where we could by no Means pursue them."[90]

Grenier argues that two elements of the strategy adapted by early colonists to counter the skulking Indians contributed to the American's "first way of war". The first element was to seek the extirpative removal of the Indians from their territory. The second element was to adapt European style warfare to the realities of the American continent. Benjamin Church argued that to defeat the Indians the colonists "must make a business of the war as the enemy did."[91] In 1676, Church enlisted the help of a group of friendly Indians to teach a group of "hardy settlers" the Indian way of skulking. That winter Church led his group into the territory of the Nipmuck Indians where they were able to successfully kill many of the enemy and return home safely. Although the expedition's success was of only limited tactical value, it did demonstrate that the

---

[88] Kretchik, *U.S. Army Doctrine: From the American Revolution to the War on Terror*, 7-8.

[89] Grenier, *The First Way of War*, 32.

[90] Nathaniel Saltonstall, *A New and Further Narrative of the State of New-England, by N.S., 1676,* in *Narratives of the Indian Wars, 1675-1699*, ed. Charles H. Lincoln (New York: Charles Scribner's Sons, 1913), 89.

[91] Benjamin Church, *Diary of King Philip's War 1675-76*, ed. Alan and Mary Simpson (Chester, CT: Pequot Press, 1975), 106.

colonists could adapt a skulking way. More importantly, according to Grenier, the Nipmuck Expedition inaugurated the tradition of the American Ranger.[92]

Church's success encouraged other colonists to establish their own groups of Rangers and they began to depend upon them for security along frontier settlements.[93] Unlike settlement militias, rangers were primarily composed of frontiersmen who traveled unencumbered through the wilderness, fought the Indians in small groups, and relied on stealth and speed rather than marching. Their methods of warfare were unconventional in European view and were often vicious in the treatment of non-combatants. Walter Kretchik described American ranger units as "notoriously independent, unit members chafed at discipline and, when fighting, shunned linear formations, preferring to exchange blows using muskets, hatchets, and knives."[94]

The informal methods of American militias and the culture of American Ranger units often clashed with the methods of British Regulars during joint campaigns. The Americans viewed the British Army as incapable of adapting their rigid doctrine to the realities of war in America while the British viewed the American militia and Rangers as "the dirtiest, the most contemptible, cowardly dogs that you can conceive."[95] The repeated failures of British Regulars during the early years of the French and Indian wars reinforced the poor opinion held by most American militias of British formalized tactics and reinforced American methods of irregular and informal warfare. However, to George Washington, the discipline of the British Army and the adaptation of its doctrine could increase the effectiveness of American militias and increase their prestige among the European powers.[96]

_____

[92] Grenier, *The First Way of War*, 32-33.

[93] The term Ranger appeared in thirteenth century England to describe foresters or borderers. To "range" is to patrol. During the seventeenth century, units titled "Border Rangers" began to appear. Church's unit provides the first evidence of the term's use in North America.

[94] Kretchik, *U.S. Army Doctrine: From the American Revolution to the War on Terror*, 8.

[95] Ibid., 9.

[96] Ibid., 10.

During the Revolutionary War, American militias demonstrated that irregular forms of warfare and informal tactics were not effective against the discipline of British regulars. Washington desired to "establish a regular system of discipline, manoeuvers, evolutions, regulations for guards &Ca. to be observed throughout the Army."[97]To do this, Washington turned to a group of European mercenaries including Steuben. Steuben quickly realized that Prussian and British doctrine would not suit the American soldier. Kretchik notes, "American soldiers were far more individualistic than their European or Atlantic counterparts …Collectively, the assembled multitude loathed physical punishment and pointless maneuvers; training required a delicate balance between Prussian discipline, British procedures, and American attitudes."[98]

Steuben's attempts to create a regulation to standardize the Continental Army were successful. On 29 March 1779, Congress approved his *Regulations for the Order and Disciple of the Troops of the United States.* Although the publication only addressed infantry units, it did enable the Continental Army to effectively maneuver against British regulars and fight alongside the regular troops of the French. By the end of the war, the regulation achieved Washington's goal of producing a cohesive army capable of matching the regular forces of European armies. However, when America proved victorious and gained its independence, the Continental Congress no longer needed the army and disbanded the organization on 2 June 1784.

The end of the Revolutionary War did not end the conflict along the frontier with the Indians. By 1789, American pioneers had established settlements along the Ohio River valley. The land the settlers occupied consisted of important hunting grounds to numerous Indian tribes. As a result, numerous bloody conflicts erupted in the newly populated territory. From June 1790 through February 1792, Congress authorized two campaigns to "extirpate marauding bands of

[97] George Washington, quoted in Walter E. Kretchik, *U.S. Army Doctrine: From the American Revolution to the War on Terror*, 14.

[98] Kretchik, *U.S. Army Doctrine: From the American Revolution to the War on Terror*, 18.

treaty-breaking Indians."[99] Both campaigns were dismal failures. Inadequate logistics, untrained militia, and adherence to inappropriate doctrine were contributing factors to the defeat of the American forces.

Success in the region came in 1793 when Major General Anthony Wayne defeated an Indian Confederacy at the Battle of Fallen Timbers. Kretchik attributes Wayne's success to his ability to adapt Steuben's *Regulations* to suit Indian combat. Using a combination of conventional and irregular tactics, Wayne was able to defeat a force of 2,000 Canadian militia and their Indian allies with only 900 men. Grenier calls Wayne "an innovative soldier who throughout his career proved capable of adapting to any situation that he faced."[100]Kretchik claims that Wayne's actions led to an enduring principle that would carry forward into future doctrine. "Fallen Timbers established that a conventional doctrine when properly applied by effective Army leadership was fully capable of defeating unconventional foes."[101]

Nineteenth century European warfare ushered in a period of radical changes in military theory. Napoleonic warfare changed both the organizational structure and method of warfare practiced by European armies. Weigley writes that the beginnings of the modern military profession began with the rise in theoretical military literature in Europe under the inspiration of Napoleon. The United States "followed these European developments and began the professionalization of its own force."[102]

During the nineteenth century, American military practitioners and theorists such as Winfield Scott, Dennis Hart Mahan, Henry Halleck, Emory Upton, John Bigelow, and Arthur L. Wagner debated and developed the doctrine that determined how Americans would train for and conduct warfare. Much of the accepted doctrine during this time was adaptions of French and

---

[99] Kretchik, *U.S. Army Doctrine: From the American Revolution to the War on Terror*, 25.

[100] Grenier, *The First Way of War*, 202.

[101] Kretchik, *U.S. Army Doctrine: From the American Revolution to the War on Terror*, 33.

[102] Weigley, *The American Way of War*, 80-81.

Prussian methods of warfare. A significant portion of these writings focused on "principles" that governed the conduct of war and the use of drill to instill discipline and control the movement of troop formations. This was particularly important in a Republican government that did not benefit from the professionalism of a large standing Army. This caused many to call for "a national system designed to accommodate both Regulars and militia, and by implication, volunteers."[103] Responding to this, in 1815, Congress approved *Infantry Tactics* as the official doctrine of the Army. This regulation would serve, with periodic modifications, as a guide for military commanders in the conduct of operations for the next four decades.

The First and Second Seminole Wars and the Mexican War each demonstrated the effectiveness of military doctrine in providing principles for the conduct of military operations. Yet each conflict also demonstrated that doctrine alone was not enough to contend with the unique realities that each situation produced. During the Seminole Wars, the doctrine allowed for the rapid movement of forces but was unable to provide guidance on how to defeat Indian tactics. To do this, military commanders had to rely on informal practices that early colonials had established to defeat local Indian populations. During the Mexican Campaign, the doctrine enabled Scott to rapidly move his Army in column and shift into line as needed. However, it failed to provide guidance on amphibious landings, sieges, or assaulting fortifications.[104] Each of these campaigns reveals that in order to conduct a successful campaign, a commander's experience, innovation and skill were required to develop innovative solutions when doctrine did not match the realities of a given conflict.[105]

---

[103] Kretchik, *U.S. Army Doctrine: From the American Revolution to the War on Terror*, 40.

[104] For a complete account of the development of *Infantry Tactics* see Kretchik, *U.S. Army Doctrine: From the American Revolution to the War on Terror*, 50-62.

[105] For a description of Scott's actions during the Mexico City Campaign and U.S. Army actions during the Seminole Wars see Timothy D. Johnson, *A Gallant Little Army: The Mexico City Campaign* (Lawrence, KS: University of Kansas Press, 2007) and John Missall and Mary Lou Missall, *The Seminole Wars: America's Longest Indian Conflict* (Gainsville, FL: University Press of Florida, 2004).

In the second half of the nineteenth century, many military theorists began to feel that American doctrine was too dependent upon European military precepts. To many, modern warfare necessitated the dispersal of troops to avoid the devastation that modern weapons had upon tight, massed formations. This meant less command control through drill and more emphasis and trust of individual training, skill of subordinates, and initiative. In 1862, Upton incorporated these thoughts into the Army's 1862 version of *Infantry Tactics*. Upton's version placed an emphasis on small units led by junior leaders. This gave the doctrine applicability to both the realities of conventional wars as well as unconventional operations against Indians.

By the 1880s, military intellectuals recognized that advancements in modern weapons had created a distinction between maneuver tactics, those required to bring a force to battle, and fighting tactics. Wagner believed that the distinction between two types of tactics coupled with Upton's emphasis on small unit tactics, stressed the importance of flexibility and initiative in the application of military principles. Wagner felt that drill was a necessary activity prior to the start of fighting but believed once the battle began, "fluidity should take precedence on the battlefield."[106] Captain A.D. Schneck also observed, "An army in battle is no longer a mere mechanical weapon in the hands of its commander" and upon engaging in battle "formal drill has vanished utterly."[107]

While Superintendent of the United States Military Academy John M. Schofield observed, "Modern changes in the tactics of battle, due to the increased range and effectiveness of firearms, bring into far greater prominence than ever before the functions of a commander…Blind obedience, courage, and even discipline, however great, can no longer be relied upon to gain victories."[108] Schofield referred to the discipline instilled by drill and the adherence to movement

---

[106] Kretchik, *U.S. Army Doctrine: From the American Revolution to the War on Terror*, 40.

[107] A.D. Schenck, "Organization of the Line of the Army," *US 13* (February 1895), 116, quoted in Brian McAllister Linn, *Echo of Battle: The Army's Way of War* (Cambridge: Harvard University Press, 2007), 63.

[108] John M. Schofield, *Forty-Six Years in the Army* (New York: The De Vinne Press, 1897), 234.

orders issued by a commander. Wagner observed that performance of drills did not demonstrate true discipline but rather the "endurance of hardships by the soldiers, and in the willing, energetic, and intelligent efforts to perform their whole duties in the presence of the enemy."[109] Wagner believed that all soldiers must possess an offensive spirit and the initiative to carry out the orders of their commanders. For the Army to succeed junior officers must be able to comprehend guidance and intent of more senior officers and be able to execute it. Linn claims that this led to the development of a form of officer he called Heroes. According to Linn, Heroes believed "It was the individual, and especially the individual commander, who was now the crucial determinant."[110]

Beginning with the publication of the Army's *Field Service Regulations (FSR)* in 1905 and continuing through the publication of *ADP 3.0* in 2011, the idea that military success is dependent upon individual initiative and an offensive spirit has been consistent in Army doctrine. Coupled with this concept is the requirement for military commanders to possess the ability to make decisions, based upon guidance from their superiors, "unperturbed by the fluctuations of combat."[111] A related theme in each of these manuals is the concept that the doctrine is only a guide to action and not a fixed set of rules. The 1939 version of FM 100-5 states, "Set rules must be avoided and methods varied. A thorough knowledge of the principles and experience in their application to various situations enable a commander to decide what methods to use in a particular situation confronting him."[112] The Army's current doctrine, *ADP 3.0*, contains the same sentiment, stating, "Doctrine acts as a guide to action rather than a set of fixed rules."[113]

---

[109] Arthur L. Wagner, *Organization and Tactics,* 6th ed. (Kansas City: Hudson-Kimberly Publishing Co., 1905), 43.

[110] Linn, *Echo of Battle*, 63.

[111] Department of the Army, *Field Service Regulation, FM 100-5: Operations* (Washington, D.C.: Headquarters Department of the Army, 1949), 17.

[112] U.S. War Department, *Field Service Regulation, FM 100-5: Operations* (Washington D.C.: Government Printing Office, 1939), II.

[113] Department of the Army, *Army Doctrine Publication 3-0: Unified Land Operations* (Washington D.C.: Headquarters Department of the Army, 2011), 1.

The American penchant for adapting, or even abandoning, doctrine to meet the realities of combat has often been a source of frustration for American opponents. German officers in World War II and Russian officers during the Cold War expressed their frustration in being unable to anticipate American actions through the study of their doctrine. Brogan claims that American disdain for pedantry infuriated both the Germans and British who had a "pathological conception of honor" and a "passion for surface fidelity to tradition and good form."[114] Brogan argues that this stems from irreverence of formal authority and a belief that "results count, where being a good loser is not thought nearly so important as being a winner, good or bad."[115]

Conclusion

The way in which Americans have conducted warfare during the past three hundred years has changed drastically. Advances in weapons, technology, communication, and society have radically altered the nature of warfare. Despite the radical changes that have occurred, some elements of how Americans conduct warfare have achieved a state of semi-permanence in both military practice and doctrine.

The ability to project power has been consistent in both military action and doctrine since early colonial operations on a rugged, wild and vast, unexplored continent. The goal of power projection has also remained relatively consistent: to move a superior force to confront an enemy. Americans have demonstrated that they prefer to meet their enemies with superior power, either in superiority in numbers, superiority in resources, superiority in technology, or preferably a combination of the three. An intelligent, adaptive commander then applies this power to reach a quick and decisive military victory by destroying the enemy army.

---

[114] Brogan, *The American Character*, 163.

[115] Ibid.

These characteristics began as military adaptations to the unique conditions experienced by early Americans. Vast distances and rugged geography, abundant natural resources and economic wealth, Republican principles and a democratic government, and rugged independence and presumed equality of it citizens all gave rise, by necessity or opportunity, to a uniquely American form of warfare. Through time, experience reinforced these adaptations and they became tendencies. Tendencies then became practice, both implicit and explicit in doctrine, and part of social and military culture.

Admittedly, the aspects of warfare presented in this monograph do not represent an all-inclusive or authoritative listing that definitively depicts the American way of warfare. Many of the challenges in characterizing a broader "way of war" also exist in characterizing a way of warfare. Warfare takes on many forms, from irregular warfare like that practiced by early colonials, to conventional battles between professional armies. Police actions, like those on the early American frontier, or peacekeeping operations, such as those in Bosnia and Kosovo, could also be included in a discussion on the forms of warfare. A listing of the characteristics of such disparate operations could be both diametrically opposed and mutually complementary, such as the depictions of an American way of war proposed by Weigley and Boot.

Accepting that there are challenges in characterizing an American way of warfare does not negate the fact that certain characteristics consistently appear in American military history, theoretical writings, and Army doctrine. Recognizing the enduring qualities of these characteristics and understanding the reasons behind their resilience is important to military leaders and planners as they face an uncertain future with undefined threats. As Shy states, "the military must ask more seriously than they have before to what extent they are dealing with learned responses which operate beneath the level of full consciousness."[116]

---

[116] Shy, "The American Military Experience," 226.

Bibliography

Biddle. Stephen. "The New Way of War? Debating the Kosovo Model." Review of *War Over Kosovo*. edited by Andrew J. Bacevich and Eliot A. Cohen. New York: Columbia University Press, 2001. and *NATO's Air War for Kosovo*. by Benjamin S. Lambeth. Santa Monica: Rand, 200.1 *Foreign Affairs* 81, no. 3 (May 1, 2002): 138.).

Boot, Max. "The New American Way of War." *Foreign Affairs* 82, no. 4 (July 1, 2003): 41-58.

Boot, Max. *The Savage Wars of Peace: Small Wars and the Rise of American Power.* New York: Basic Books, 2002.

Bradford, James C., ed. *A Companion to American Military History,* vol. 2. Oxford: Blackwell Publishing Ltd, 2010.

Brogan, D.W. *The American Character.* New York: Alfred A. Knopf, 1944.

Bruner, Jerome S., Goodnow, Jacqueline J, and Austin, George A. *A Study of Thinking.* New York: Wiley, 1956.

Bruscino, Thomas A, "Our American Mind for War." Review of *The Echo of Battle: The Army's Way of War*. Brian McAllister Linn. Cambridge, MA: Harvard University Press, 2007. The Claremont Institute. http://www.claremont.org/publications/pub_print.asp?pubid=762 (accessed September 8, 2011).

Cebrowski, Arthur K, and Thomas P M Barnett. "The American Way of War." United States Naval Institute. Proceedings, January 1, 2003, 42-43. http://www.proquest.com.lumen.cgsccarl.com/ (accessed August 11, 2011).

Church, Benjamin. *Diary of King Philip's War 1675-76.* Edited by Alan and Mary Simpson. Chester, CT: Pequot Press, 1975.

Clausewitz, Carl Von. *On War.* Translated and edited by Michael Howard and Peter Paret. Princeton: Princeton University Press, 1976.

Center for Military History. *War in the Persian Gulf: Operations Desert Shield and Desert Storm August 1990 – March 1991.* Washington, D.C.: U.S. Army Center for Military History, 2010.

Command and General Staff School. *The Principles of Strategy for an Independent Corps.* Fort Leavenworth, KS: The Command and General Staff School Press, 1936.

Cunliffe, Marcus. *Soldiers & Civilians: The Martial Spirit in America, 1775-1865.* New York: The Free Press, 1973.

Echevarria, Antulio J.II. *After Clausewitz:German Military Thinkers Before the Great War.* Lawrence, KS: University Press of Kansas, 2000.

Echevarria, Antulio J.II. "Toward an American Way of War." Strategic Studies Institute, March 2004. http://permanent.access.gpo.gov/websites/armymil/www.carlisle.army.mil/ssi/pdffiles/00 365.pdf (accessed August 11, 2011).

Ferling, John. *A Wilderness of Miseries: War and Warriors in Early America.* Westport,CT: Greenwood Press, 1980.

Gafney, H.H. "The American Way of War Through 2020." Alexandria, VA: Center for Strategic Studies, CNA Corporation, 2006.

Gray, Colin S. "National Style in Strategy: The American Example." *International Security,* Vol. 6, No. 2 (Autumn, 1981), 21-47.

Gray, Colin S. *War, Peace, and International Relations: An Introduction to Strategic History.* New York: Rutledge, 2007.

Grenier, John. *The First Way of War: American War Making on the Frontier, 1607-1814.* Cambridge: Cambridge University Press, 2005.

Hanson, Victor Davis. "The American way of war." *National Review,* (April 21, 2003), 10.

Hanson, Victor Davis. *Carnage and Culture.* New York: Anchor Books, 2001.

Harrison, Gordon A. *Cross-Channel Attack.* Washington, D.C.: U.S. Army Center of Military History, 1993.

Hart, B.H. Liddell. *Strategy.* New York: Frederick A. Praeger, 1956.

Higginbotham, Don "The Early American Way of War: Reconnaissance and Appraisal," *The William and Mary Quarterly,* Third Series, Vol. 44, No. 2 (April, 1987).

Johnson, Timothy D. *A Gallant Little Army: The Mexicon City Campaign.* Lawrence, KS: University of Kansas Press, 2007.

Karr, Ronald Dale. "Why Should You Be So Ferocious?: The Violence of the Pequot War," *Journal of American History*, 85 (1999).

Keravuori, Rose Lopez. "Lost in Translation: The American Way of War." *Small Wars Journal* (November, 2011).

Kirkpatrick, Charles E. *An Unknown Future and Doubtful Present: Writing the Victory Plan of 1941.* Washington, D.C.: U.S. Army Center of Military History, 1992.

Kretchik, Walter E. *U.S. Army Doctrine: From the American Revolution to the War on Terror.* Lawrence, KS: University Press of Kansas, 2011.

Linn, Brian M. "The American Way of War revisited." *The Journal of Military History* 66, no. 2 (April 1, 2002): 501.

Linn, Brian M. *The Echo of Battle: The Army's Way of War.* Cambridge, MA: Harvard University Press, 2007.

Lynn, John A. *Battle: A History of Combat and Culture, From Ancient Greece to Modern Times.* New York: Basic Books, 2003.

Milner, Marc. "In Search of the American Way of War: The Need for a Wider National and International Context." *The Journal of American History* 93, no. 4 (March 1, 2007): 1151-1153.

Missall, John and Missall, Mary Lou. *The Seminole Wars: America's Longest Indian Conflict.* Gainesville, FL: University Press of Florida, 2004.

Myers, Richard B. "The New American Way of War." *Military Technology*, (June 1, 2003), 64.

Naylor, William K. *Principles of Strategy with Historical Illustrations.* Fort Leavenworth, KS: The General Service Schools, 1921.

Nelson , Paul David. *Anthony Wayne: Soldier of the Early Republic.* Bloomington, IN: Indiana University Press, 1985.

Parker, Geoffrey, ed. *Cambridge Illustrated History: Warfare.* Cambridge, NY: Cambridge University Press, 1995.

Pickering, Timothy. *An Easy Plan of Discipline for a Militia.* Salem, MA: Samuel and Ebenezer Hall, 1775.

Record, Jeffrey. "The American Way of War: Cultural Barriers to Successful Counterinsurgency." September 1, 2006. http://www.cato.org/pub_display.php?pub_id=6640 (accessed August 11, 2011).

Roosevelt, Franklin D. *The American Way: Selections from the Public Addresses and Papers of Franklin D. Roosevelt.* Edited by Dagobert D.Runes. New York: Philosophical Library, 1944.

Saltonstall, Nathaniel. *A New and Further Narrative of the State of New-England, by N.S., 1676,* in *Narratives of the Indian Wars, 1675-1699.* Edited by Charles H. Lincoln. New York: Charles Scribner's Sons, 1913.

Schofield, John M. *Forty-Six Years in the Army.* New York: The De Vinne Press, 1897.

Schwarzkopf, H. Norman and Petre, Peter. *It Doesn't Take a Hero.* New York: Bantam Books, 1992.

Shaw, Martin. *The New Western Way of War.* Cambridge, UK: Polity Press, 2005.

Shaw, Martin. *Dialectics of War.* London: Pluto Publishing Ltd, 1988.

Shy, John. "The American Military Experience: History and Learning." *The Journal of Interdisciplinary History,* Vol. 1, No. 2 (Winter, 1971), 205-228.

Snider, Don M. "America's Postmodern Military." *World Policy Journal* 17, no. 1 (April 1, 2000): 47-54.

The Command and General Staff School. *The Principles of Strategy for an Independent Corps or Army in a Theater of Operations.* Fort Leavenworth, KS: The Command and General Staff School Press, 1936.

The General Service Schools. *Review of Current Military Writings* no. 19. (October-December, 1925): 20.

U.S. Department of the Army. *Field Service Regulation, FM 100-5: Operations.* Washington D.C.: U.S. Government Printing Office, 1949.

U.S. Department of the Army. *Field Service Regulation, FM 100-5: Operations.* Washington D.C.: U.S. Government Printing Office, 1954.

U.S. Department of the Army. *Field Service Regulation, FM 100-5: Operations.* Washington, D.C.: Headquarters Department of the Army, 1962.

U.S. Department of the Army. *Field Manual 100-5: Operations.* Washington, D.C.: Headquarters Department of the Army, 1982.

U.S. Department of the Army. *Field Manual 100-5: Operations.* Washington, D.C.: Headquarters Department of the Army, 1986.

U.S. Department of the Army. *Field Manual 100-5: Operations.* Washington, D.C.: Headquarters Department of the Army, 1993.

U.S. War Department. *Field Service Regulation, FM 100-5: Operations.* Washington D.C.: Government Printing Office, 1939.

U.S. War Department. *Field Service Regulation, FM 100-5: Operations.* Washington D.C.: Government Printing Office, 1941.

Wagner, Arthur L. *Organization and Tactics,* 6th ed. Kansas City: Hudson-Kimberly Publishing Co., 1905.

Washington, George. *The Writings of George Washington, 1745-1799.* Edited by John C. Fitzpatrick. Washington, DC: Government printing Office, 1931-1944.

Weigley, Russell F. *The American Way of War: A History of United States Military Strategy and Policy.* Bloomington, IN: Indiana University Press, 1973.

Weigley, Russell F. *The Age of Battles: The Quest for Decisive Warfare from Breitenfeld to Waterloo.* Bloomington, IN: Indiana University Press, 1991.

Weigley, Russell F. *Eisenhower's Lieutenants: The Campaign of France and Germany 1944-1945.* Bloomington, IN: Indiana University Press, 1981.